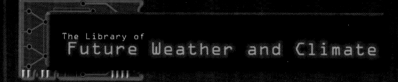

The Library of
Future Weather and Climate

Biomes
of the Future

Paul Stein

The Rosen Publishing Group, Inc.
New York

Published in 2001 by The Rosen Publishing Group, Inc.
29 East 21st Street, New York, NY 10010

First Edition

Library of Congress Cataloging-in-Publication Data

Stein, Paul, 1968–
Biomes of the future / Paul Stein.
p. cm. — (The library of future weather and climate)
Includes bibliographical references and index.
ISBN 0-8239-3410-1 (lib. bdg.)
1. Bioclimatology—Juvenile literature. 2. Global temperature changes—
Environmental aspects—Juvenile literature. [1. Bioclimatology.
2. Climatic changes. 3. Biotic communities.] I. Title.
QH543 .S74 2001
577.2'2—dc21

2001000137

All temperatures in this book are in degrees Fahrenheit, except where specifically noted. To convert to degrees Celsius, or centigrade, use the following formula:

Celsius temperature = (5 ÷ 9) x (the temperature in Fahrenheit - 32)

Manufactured in the United States of America

Contents

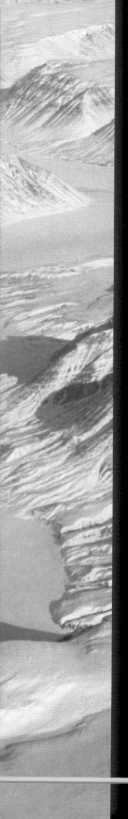

Introduction

One thousand two hundred miles north of the nearest tree, Ellesmere Island sits nestled up against the northwestern shoulder of Greenland. It's the northernmost outcrop of land in Canada. Beyond its icy shores lies the Arctic Ocean, with the North Pole less than 500 miles distant. Ellesmere Island is very nearly the end of the world.

The craggy shoreline is split by fjords, long narrow inlets of sea flanked by steep cliffs. Glacier-draped mountains rise over 8,000 feet above the interior of the island. The rocky, icy landscape covers over 15,000 square miles. So desolate is this part of the world that NASA has come here for experiments that test the endurance of future Mars exploration vehicles.

Fossil records indicate that Ellesmere Island was once warm enough for alligators and other warm-weather creatures. Today, Ellesmere is far too cold for alligators.

Life struggles to survive here. The short, bleak summer allows nothing more than some tiny wildflowers to emerge from between the rocks. Herds of musk oxen roam the desolate terrain, along with the occasional wolf or fox. A few rabbits and birds add to the thin mixture of species. Snowdrifts remain throughout summer, as temperatures often struggle to rise above freezing. In the winter, months of total darkness and temperatures well below zero drive most living things underground or south.

It's not the kind of place in which you would expect to find alligators. But Ellesmere Island, high in the Arctic, has them. These are not live alligators; they are fossils, over 50 million years old. Scientists have also found other kinds of fossilized animals on Ellesmere, including ancient turtles. And in 1985 on nearby Axel Heiberg Island, scientists discovered the remains of a 45-million-year-old forest. Over 1,000 stumps and trunks from ancient trees that probably stood as high as 150 feet litter the now-treeless landscape. There are ancient relatives of modern-day redwood, sycamore, chestnut, spruce, and pine, along with the remains of leaves and pinecones, dead for millions of years, but preserved in the frigid Arctic.

Alligators need an average annual temperature of at least 59°F to survive. Today in North America, they are found only in the southern United States, in places like Florida, Louisiana, Texas, and the southernmost part of Georgia. It appears, therefore, that frigid Ellesmere Island once supported a warm, swampy, forest biome. Simply put, a biome is a large collection of plants and animals living under common climatic and geographic conditions. While Ellesmere's biome today is classified as tundra, with average annual temperatures below freezing, 50 million years ago things were very different.

A logical but mistaken explanation for the drastically different ancient environment on Ellesmere is that the island was not always located so far north. The earth's crust is divided into plates, which jostle and move over time. Over tens of millions of years, the earth's land masses can rearrange themselves. A land area that is in a warm part of the world, closer to the equator, may over long periods of time move into a colder part of the world closer to the poles. However, scientists think that Ellesmere Island has for millions of

Millions of years ago, Earth's overall climate was much warmer than it is today.

years remained just about where it is today, high in the Arctic, facing the North Pole—hardly the kind of place where you would expect to find a swamp.

The most likely explanation for the alligators of Ellesmere is that the climate of the earth was significantly different 50 million years ago. At that time, experts think that the earth was much warmer. Today, the difference in average annual temperature between the North Pole and the equator is as much as 45°F. Back then, scientists speculate that the difference in temperature was only 9°F. It was a greenhouselike world, with tropical warmth that extended far from the equator. Palm trees grew where the city of Chicago now stands, and alligators roamed the islands north of the Arctic Circle.

Evidence from history shows that climate strongly influences where plants and animals live on the planet. These arrangements of living organisms, called biomes, evolve over time within the thresholds of weather. Each different species of plant and animal adapts to survive in certain ranges of temperature, rainfall, snowfall, and wind.

Entering the twenty-first century, we face the fastest rate of global climate change in 10,000 years. Global warming, brought on by increasing levels of greenhouse gases in the atmosphere, threatens to bring unprecedented change to the earth's weather over the next century and beyond. The effects of changing climate will be many. Of these effects, the possible consequences for plants and animals are of major concern. In fact, many researchers are now seeing startling changes in biomes, likely brought on by climate changes that are already under way.

Before we examine how changes in the earth's climate might affect plants and animals, we must first explore biomes. From Arctic tundra to tropical rain forests, life on Earth has organized itself into common groups. Each group, or biome, has its unique characteristics. Each is essential for the diversity of the planet, each a pattern in the tapestry of life into which humans are woven.

1 Biomes of the World

Sprawling like a thick, moist, green carpet across the interior of northern South America, the Amazon rain forest covers over two million square miles. That's more than half the size of the entire United States. Within the dense jungle lives the most abundant concentration of plants and animals on the planet. Several million different kinds of organisms call the Amazon rain forest home, and some species still remain undiscovered.

The sheer number of species is extraordinary. Biologists estimate that one square mile of Amazon jungle can contain over 100 different kinds of trees. A typical forest in the United States, by contrast, might offer three to five species

Water draining out of the Amazon rain forest flows into the 4,000-mile-long Amazon River.

of trees in the same area. It's estimated that the Amazon holds 1,600 species of birds and over a million different kinds of insects—with as many as 30,000 crawling around on (and in) one large tree alone.

In the highest tree tops, colorful butterflies dance from leaf to leaf. Exotic birds perch and swoop, feeding on insects. Farther down, other species live in the dense canopy layer of the jungle. This is the thick layer of treetops that covers the jungle as high as 150 feet up, letting through relatively little light. Birds and butterflies are found in abundance here, too, along with bats and other smaller mammals. Certain species of snakes slither among the canopy branches and leaves in search of a meal. Deeper down into the middle layer of forest, at a height of 20 to 50 feet or so, monkeys jump from vine to vine. Tree frogs cling to the sides of trees. Panthers sometimes scale smaller trees to find food. Other small mammals roam the shrubs on the forest floor. Large colonies of ants and termites make their homes in the soil or in rotting tree trunks. Most of the time, the air is dripping with humidity. Frequent tropical cloudbursts keep everything wet. Water draining out of the rain forest flows into the 4,000-mile-long Amazon River, the second longest river in the world.

A rain forest, such as the one found in the Amazon, is a kind of biome. It's a unique blend of plants and animals that have adapted to the hot and humid regional climate. In general, the world's tropical rain forests are found between 23.5 degrees north and south latitude, or within about 1,700 miles of the equator. There are no real seasons in tropical rain forests, though most rain forests cycle through the year between wetter and drier periods. Temperatures generally fall no lower than 70°F and rise not much higher than the low 90s. Tropical rain forests are among the wettest places on Earth, typically receiving over 150 inches of rain each year.

The rain forest is home to many different creatures, including numerous species of snakes.

Rain forests can also be found outside the tropics. These nontropical regions are often called temperate zones and lie in the Northern and Southern Hemispheres between the colder Arctic and the warmer Tropics. The United States is situated in a temperate zone. Temperate rain

forests, such as the one found on the Olympic Peninsula in Washington State, also receive extraordinary amounts of rainfall. But they're much cooler than their tropical counterparts, with temperatures that rarely rise above 80 degrees or sink below freezing.

Most of the forest biomes in temperate regions are not rain forests. Temperate forests cover much of the eastern part of the United States and central and eastern Europe. Temperatures in this kind of biome can vary widely, from -40°F to over 100°F. Annual precipitation is moderate, ranging generally from thirty to sixty inches, and is distributed fairly evenly through the year. In contrast to rain forests, which have dense canopies, the canopy of temperate forests is moderately dense and allows more light to penetrate to the forest floor.

Common tree species in temperate forests include oak, hickory, beech, hemlock, maple, cottonwood, elm, willow, and a variety of pine trees. Different kinds of mammals live in temperate forests, including squirrels, rabbits, skunks, deer, wolves, and bears. Rarer are the mountain lion, bobcat, and timber wolf. Birds are found in abundance, though in general the diversity of plant and animal life in temperate forests is much less than it is in tropical rain forests.

The third kind of forest biome is called taiga, or boreal forest. These are the great northern forests that extend across large parts of Canada, Alaska, Russia, and Scandinavia. In fact, the taiga is the largest land-based biome on the planet. Precipitation in the taiga is generally lower than it is in temperate forests, usually ranging from fifteen to twenty-five inches per year. A relatively large portion of the precipitation that falls in these northern forests is in the form of snow, owing to the long winter season and much lower temperatures. In the winter, readings can drop to -50°F, while summertime temperatures rarely rise above 55°F.

Boreal forests are characterized by abundant conifers. A conifer is a tree that carries cones, such as fir trees and pine trees. Animals in the taiga include brown and grizzly bears, moose, lynx, foxes, deer, wolves, elk, rabbits, weasels, chipmunks, and a variety of birds, including larger predatory birds like eagles and hawks. Mosquitoes and blackflies swarm through the taiga in spring after the ground thaws and the temperature rises.

Some kinds of biomes have relatively few trees. Grasslands, for example, are relatively treeless biomes that cover large parts of tropical and temperate regions. In the Tropics, grasslands are called savannas. Savannas cover nearly half of Africa, as well as large parts of Australia and South America. Average annual rainfall typically ranges from twenty to fifty inches, most of which falls during a well-defined "wet" season. Temperatures are on the high side, generally from the 70s to the 90s. Temperate grasslands, on the other hand, have much more extreme temperatures and lower rainfall than savannas. Average yearly precipitation is generally no more than thirty-five inches and can be as low as ten inches. Temperatures rise over 100°F at times during the summer and drop as low as -40°F in the winter. Temperate grasslands are categorized either as prairies,

Temperate rain forests, such as those on the Olympic Peninsula in Washington State, receive large amounts of rainfall but are cooler than their tropical counterparts.

with longer grasses, or steppes, with shorter grasses. Both prairies and steppes are found over large parts of central North America, central Asia, and small sections of southern South America, South Africa, and southeastern Australia.

.   Grasslands are home to a wide variety of wildlife. In Africa, for instance, the savanna serves as a habitat for giraffes, elephants, rhinoceroses, zebras, and wildebeests, among other species. The big cats, such as lions, leopards, and cheetahs, stalk their prey here. Ostriches, jackals, and hyenas add to the diversity. Termites build dirt mounds that can rise over ten feet high. The few trees

The African savanna is home to grazing animals and the big cats that stalk them.

that grow in grasslands include acacia trees and the baobab. Wildfires sweep through grasslands each year and are an important component of the natural growing cycle.

A more extreme kind of biome is the desert. Here, life struggles to survive in some of the world's most brutal climatic conditions. Annual rainfall in deserts is often less than ten inches, and some of the world's deserts are so dry that they can go for years without a drop of rain. Temperatures soar as high as 130°F in the hottest deserts but can also plunge into the 30s at night. Hot deserts, such as the Sahara, lie near the equator. Colder deserts, like the Gobi Desert in central Asia and the Great Basin in the western United States, lie outside the Tropics and have much lower average temperatures. Other great desert regions of the world include western and central Australia, the southwestern United States and northern Mexico, the Arabian Peninsula, southwestern Africa, and parts of western South America. In all, deserts cover some 20 percent of Earth's land surface.

Because of the harsh and often blistering daytime weather conditions, life in the desert usually comes out at night. Reptiles, such as snakes and lizards, are night hunters. So are the arachnids, such as spiders and scorpions. Small mammals and birds are active at night as well. Most animals seek shelter from the daytime heat under rocks or in burrows. Plant life is minimal in the desert and consists mostly of cacti, flowers, and small shrubs that need little water for survival.

The Arctic is also sometimes characterized as a desert biome because so little precipitation falls there. But the official name given to the treeless, barren, and cold Arctic biome is tundra. Tundra extends from Alaska across northern Canada and across northern Asia. It's bordered to the south by the taiga, the large northern boreal forests, and on the north by the Arctic Ocean. Like the desert, it's a place of extremes. Summertime temperatures typically rise no higher than the 50s, and snow can fall through all twelve months of the year. The Sun sets on the tundra in autumn and does not rise again until spring. In the icy darkness of winter, temperatures regularly plunge below -50°F.

The tundra harbors a very low diversity of life. Ellesmere Island, described in the introduction, is an example of a tundra biome. Moss, lichen, and small flowers are the primary kinds of plant life here. Migrating herds of caribou and musk oxen share the landscape with lemmings, voles, hares, foxes, wolves, and the occasional polar bear. Mosquitoes and flies breed in the fleeting summer warmth. Falcons, snow buntings, sandpipers, terns, and gulls are some of the species of birds that inhabit the tundra.

A tundralike biome can also exist at the tops of mountains much farther to the south. In general, the higher the altitude, the lower the air temperature. High mountain peaks, such as those in the Rocky Mountains, the Alps, and the Himalayas, therefore, have very different biomes than surrounding lower-elevation areas. These mountain biomes are called alpine, after the European mountain chain. Goats, sheep, elk, birds, and hardy insects inhabit the alpine biome. On these cold, windswept elevations, trees become scarce and stunted. Grasses and wildflowers grow in abundance.

The last major kind of biome is the aquatic biome. This includes all freshwater lakes, ponds, streams, and rivers, along with the world's saltwater oceans. In all, water covers around 75 percent of the earth's surface and is home to an extraordinary diversity of life. From trout and salmon to sharks, dolphins, and whales, fish and mammals both call the water home. Crustaceans, like crabs, lobsters, and crawfish, inhabit the rocky, shallow bottoms of freshwater and saltwater biomes. Vast beds of coral bloom in the warm, tropical waters of the world. Mollusks, like clams and mussels, cling to rocks that are alternately covered and uncovered by the rising and falling tide. Ducks and birds flock through coastal regions and wetlands by the thousands. Grasses, lilies, and water-loving trees such as mangroves are just some of the plants found in aquatic biomes. Microscopic plankton are perhaps the most important, serving as the most fundamental aquatic food source. It is estimated that aquatic biomes are home to as much as 30 percent of all plant and animal species on Earth.

The variety of biomes across the planet are not situated randomly. Rather, they owe their existence to long-term, average weather conditions that vary from region to region. Next, we look at how climate shapes the land and the plants and animals that live upon it.

2 Biomes and the Weather

What causes certain kinds of biomes to be located where they are? Why, for instance, are most of the world's deserts located in two distinct zones, around 30 degrees north and south latitude? The answer has to do with the way air circulates around the planet. The global circulation of air sets up certain kinds of weather patterns over various regions of the world. Biomes develop over long periods of time as plants and animals adapt to these local weather conditions.

The pattern of circulating air around the earth is determined in part by the uneven heating of the earth by the Sun. Sunlight strikes the earth much more indirectly at the poles than it does at the equator. The polar regions, therefore, are

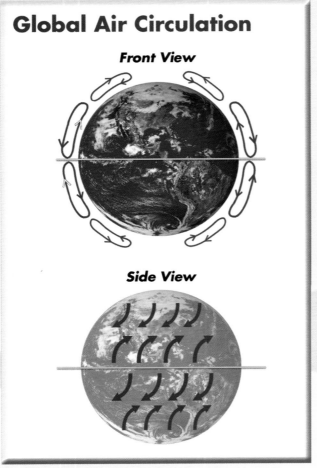

Global Air Circulation

Front View

Side View

The rotation of the earth bends air currents flowing north and south to the right.

the coldest parts of the planet while the equator is the warmest. Essentially, air moves in an attempt to compensate for this temperature difference. Cold air from the poles moves south toward the Tropics, and warm air from the Tropics moves north toward the poles. As air moves, its direction is altered by the spinning of the earth underneath it. This spinning motion causes windflow to curve toward the right in the Northern Hemisphere and toward the left in the Southern Hemisphere. While there are other forces that act on air, essentially air moves around the world to equalize the global temperature imbalance. In so doing, it has developed a distinct pattern of circulation.

While there is no beginning or ending point in this circulation, one place to start when describing the global circulation is the Tropics. Air warmed by the Sun near the equator tends to expand

and rise as the air molecules move faster and become less dense. As air rises, it carries tropical humidity skyward, forming clouds, showers, and thunderstorms. To replace this rising air in the Tropics, other air flows in horizontally near the earth's surface from the northeast and southeast. These winds are known as the trade winds. The zone of rising air and clouds into which the trade winds flow is known as the intertropical convergence zone, or ITCZ. The ITCZ extends around the earth near the equator, like a belt.

The ITCZ shapes tropical biomes by delivering abundant rainfall. From Brazil to central Africa to the islands of southeastern Asia, tropical rain forests thrive in the high humidity, rainfall, and heat beneath the intertropical convergence zone. As the ITCZ shifts northward or southward through the year, the tropical rain forests receive more or less rainfall. These wet and less-wet times of the year are the only kind of seasonal weather change the Tropics experience.

High in the sky over the Tropics, the air that rises along the ITCZ eventually hits a layer of warmer, stable air called the stratosphere. The stratosphere is a stable layer of air because it acts like a lid, preventing air from moving upward or downward. Air rising from below hits the stratosphere and is forced to spread out horizontally toward the north and the south. As this horizontally spreading air flows hundreds of miles toward the poles, it slowly converges, or comes together. Looking at a globe, it's easy to see why air converges as it flows toward the north. Follow the north-south longitude lines, and see how they come closer together the farther north or south you get.

Sinking air in the sub-Tropics has created a vast desert region from northern Africa to the Arabian Peninsula.

The poleward moving air also becomes cooler as it moves out of the Tropics. As the air converges and cools, its density increases, causing it to sink back down toward the surface of the earth. This sinking air occurs in the sub-Tropics near 30 degrees north and south latitude. As the sinking air hits the earth's surface, it spreads apart horizontally. Some of the air moves southward, eventually flowing into the Tropics and rising again along the ITCZ.

The zone of sinking air around 30 degrees north and south latitude marks the favored location of the world's desert biomes. Clouds and rainfall form where air rises (such as along the ITCZ), while sinking air tends to favor clear skies and dry weather. Year after year, century after century, sinking air in the sub-Tropics has dried out the land. In the Northern Hemisphere, a vast desert region centered around 30 degrees north latitude extends from northern Africa to the Arabian Peninsula. In the

Southern Hemisphere, major deserts are found at 30 degrees south latitude in South America, southwestern Africa, and Australia. These desert biomes attest to the persistent, cloud- and rain-hindering weather pattern in these parts of the world.

Some of the air that sinks in the sub-Tropics hits the earth and spreads northeastward. Meanwhile, near the poles, dense cold air sinks and spreads southeast. The air moving southeast from the poles collides with the air moving northeast from the sub-Tropics along a boundary called the polar front. The position of this front varies by season, and it undulates northward and southward as weather systems move across the temperate zones. As air collides along the polar front, it rises, cools, and expands once again. Moisture in the rising, cooling air condenses into clouds that produce rain or snow.

The temperate zones, therefore, are the battleground for warm air moving north from the sub-Tropics and cold air moving south from the poles. Great swirling storms form and decay over days and weeks along the polar front, which is really a discontinuous boundary between warm air to the south and cold air to the north. The clouds, rain, and snow along the polar front supply biomes in the temperate zones with moisture fairly evenly throughout the year.

Because of the periodic wet weather in the temperate zones, extreme biomes like rain forests and deserts are rarer here. Where they do occur, their existence is related not so much to the global circulation of air, but to the land itself, or to the oceans. Ocean water is the source for most of the atmospheric moisture that produces clouds and precipitation. But land features, such as large mountain ranges, can block the flow of air from the oceans in certain regions and give rise to a dry environment. In other places, direct access to ocean moisture makes for a much wetter environment.

Washington State, in the Pacific Northwest region of the United States, has within its borders a striking example of two contrasting biomes shaped by the relationship between land and ocean. On the Olympic Peninsula of western Washington, moisture-laden air sweeps inland from the Pacific Ocean. While regularly occurring storm systems drop heavy amounts of precipitation here, especially in the winter, coastal mountains make the weather even wetter. As the wet air flows inland, it hits the mountains and rises upward. Since rising air promotes the growth of clouds and rain, the ocean-facing slopes of coastal mountains are especially wet places. In fact, the Olympic Peninsula in Washington State receives over 200 inches of rain per year. That's about five times the amount that Seattle receives, only seventy-five miles to the east. Not surprisingly, a temperate rain forest biome thrives on the rain-drenched coastal mountain slopes.

Just east of Seattle, the Cascade Range rises over 10,000 feet in a north-south line from the border of Canada into Oregon. The Cascades act as a barrier to inland-flowing moist ocean air. While clouds and rain dampen areas west of the Cascades, areas east of the Cascades are often rain free. Annual precipitation amounts in lower elevations of western Washington commonly range from

The Cascades are barriers to inland-flowing ocean air. On the eastern side of the Cascades, there are desert and grassland biomes, and on the western side, there is a rain forest biome.

forty to fifty inches. Only a hundred miles on the other side of the mountains, however, annual precipitation is only eight to twelve inches. Thus there exist water-scarce desert and grassland biomes on the eastern side of the Cascades, and a waterlogged rain forest biome on the western side.

The relationship between land features and ocean moisture exerts a strong impact on biomes, especially in temperate zones. Elsewhere, biomes owe their existence to persistent weather patterns that arise from the global circulation of air. In the next chapter we discuss how the global climate is changing and how this change in climate might affect the biomes of the world.

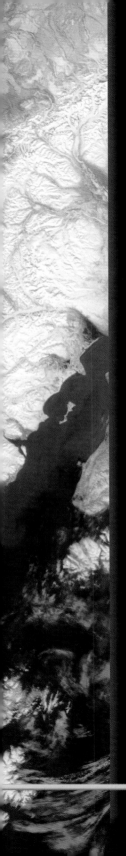

3 The Global Greenhouse

Locals call it the "drunken forest." In Alaska, stands of trees lean at crazy angles. What once were straight, tall, sturdy taiga spruce are now diseased, dying, and tilted in all directions. Swampy ponds flood the forest floor underneath the once-mighty trees. In the Arctic, the ground is melting.

Across most of Alaska, a layer of permafrost lies just underneath the surface of the earth. Permafrost is a layer of soil that stays frozen year-round. Since the ground and the air above it must be very cold to keep the soil frozen, permafrost occurs only in high latitudes—for instance, northern Canada, Alaska, and Russia. Scientists estimate that permafrost underlies anywhere from 13 percent to 25 percent of the world's land surface. It can be up to a thousand feet thick in places.

The northern taiga forest biome grows on top of this permafrost layer. The root systems of trees in the taiga cannot penetrate the permafrost and remain in the shallow layer of unfrozen soil just below ground level. If, for any reason, the permafrost melts, the land above it sinks down into the wet, spongelike earth. Shallow-rooted trees growing above melting permafrost lean wildly as the ground sinks unevenly. Many of the trees weaken and die. Thus, the forest becomes "drunken."

According to the Geologic Survey of Canada, the permafrost in parts of that country has retreated northward by over fifty miles in the last century. Many experts take it as another sign of global warming, the name given to the long-term warming trend in the earth's atmosphere. Other indications of changing climate in Arctic regions include melting glaciers and river ice that breaks apart earlier and earlier each spring.

In recent years, scientists have been paying increasing attention to the influence of human activity on the earth's climate, in particular, the burning of fossil fuels and the effect this has on the average global temperature. Fossil fuels include coal, natural gas, and oil. They're so-named because they are created deep underground over millions of years from the fossilized remains of plants. Plants, like all life, are based on carbon molecules. When we burn fossil fuels to make energy, therefore, we release this carbon into the atmosphere in the form of carbon dioxide (CO_2), a gas. Since the late seventeenth and early eighteenth centuries, when coal was first used in large volume to drive the Industrial Revolution, CO_2 amounts in the earth's atmosphere have increased by 30 percent. And with the gigantic energy needs of the

When we burn fossil fuels such as coal, natural gas, and oil to make energy, we release CO_2 gas, which warms the atmosphere. This warming has a profound effect on the earth's climate.

modern world, more and more CO_2 is being pumped into the atmosphere every day. Cars and trucks that run on gasoline release CO_2 into the air through their exhaust. Most power plants that supply the electricity needed to turn on lights, or anything else that uses electricity, generate power through the burning of fossil fuels. Our modern society has been largely built by the combustion of ancient plants.

It turns out, however, that carbon dioxide has a profound effect on the earth's climate. CO_2 is known as a greenhouse gas. This means that it is an efficient absorber of a certain kind of energy called radiation. Radiation consists of invisible electromagnetic waves that travel at the speed of light. Everything both gives off and absorbs radiation. The temperature of an object depends on the amount of radiation the object absorbs compared to the amount it gives off. If an object absorbs more radiation than it receives, it warms. If it gives off more radiation than it absorbs, it cools.

Carbon dioxide and other greenhouse gases, such as methane, water vapor, and chlorofluorocarbons, warm the atmosphere by absorbing radiation given off by the earth. The more of these greenhouse gases in the air, the more energy is absorbed and the warmer the atmosphere becomes. Scientists estimate that the average temperature of the earth was at least 1°F warmer at the end of the twentieth century than at the beginning. Though a difference of one degree seems small, it's significant considering the average planetary temperature has increased only by five to nine degrees since the last ice age. Furthermore, the rate of temperature rise is accelerating. The warmest years of the twentieth century all occurred in the 1980s and 1990s. In particular, the 1990s were not only the warmest decade of the twentieth century, but scientists think in all likelihood it was the warmest decade of the last 1,000 years. And while some debate still exists between experts on the cause of the recent global warming, many scientists think that some of it—perhaps most of it—is due to the increase in greenhouse gases in the atmosphere. By looking at current trends, including the rate of rising CO_2 levels, and using this data to run extremely complex simulations of the atmosphere and oceans, scientists think that the earth could warm by three to nearly eleven additional degrees over the next century.

There are three main ways that global warming can affect, and possibly threaten, the world's biomes. The first is by causing regional changes in temperature, rainfall, and snowfall. Since biomes are so closely linked to regional climate and weather patterns, global warming stands to exert a profound impact on plant and animal life around the world. The drunken forest in Alaska (and in other Arctic regions) is just one example of how a warming atmosphere can cause damage to a biome.

As air temperatures rise and rainfall patterns change, plants and animals that have adapted to a regional climate over hundreds of thousands of years will be forced to adapt or to migrate. Adapting is a slow process. Experts think the magnitude of climate change in the twenty-first century will be as great as the amount of climate change that has taken place since the last ice age, 20,000 years ago. Some species may not be able to adapt to new weather conditions fast enough.

Global warming threatens plants and animals in alpine biomes on mountains. These species can live only in cold areas; if the climate warms, they may have to migrate or adapt, or face extinction.

At particular risk are plant and animal species in alpine biomes on mountains. Certain kinds of plants and animals have carved out their own niches in relatively cold, mountaintop environments. If the climate warms, the only place for them to migrate is upward. At some point during the warming process, mountain-dwelling species will run out of room. Some species may become extinct.

At lower elevations, northward migration also has its limits. Experts think that a two to six degree change in the average temperature of the earth would cause climate zones to shift northward by 100 to 350 miles. For example, the location in the United States where the average July high temperature is 85°F will move up to 350 miles northward. That's about the distance from Philadelphia, Pennsylvania, to Portland, Maine. Since animals are more mobile, they would be better able to keep up with this change in climate. Plants, however, migrate much more slowly. And the ease at which both plants and animals can relocate is severely restricted in some places by human development. Cities, suburbs, and highways all impose artificial barriers to the movement of species within a biome. As the planet warms, some species will be blocked from migrating with the climate.

When it comes to plant life, there may actually be a thin silver lining to the otherwise gloomy global-warming cloud. The growing season will last longer farther north in a warmed world. Certain kinds of crops may be grown where they have never thrived before. Also, trees and plants may grow faster and larger because of what's known as the fertilization effect. Using sunlight, trees and plants convert CO_2 and water into plant material through the process of photosynthesis. The more CO_2 in the air, the more efficient this process becomes. This is the second way that global warming may affect biomes.

Scientists have done some preliminary studies of the fertilization effect on a temperate forest biome. Researchers at Duke University in North Carolina examined the growth rates and behavior of pine trees when subjected to higher-than-normal carbon dioxide levels. They pumped 150 percent of present-day CO_2 concentrations into the air over a ninety-foot diameter tract of North Carolina pine forest. For comparison, they also studied similar areas of forest where carbon dioxide levels remained unchanged. They found that trees

Trees and plants are a vital part of all of the earth's biomes. Plants convert CO$_2$ into oxygen, which animals and humans need to survive.

exposed to higher carbon dioxide levels yielded twice as many pinecones as the untreated trees. Some people point to the carbon dioxide fertilization effect as a positive aspect of global warming. However, in a warmer world, fertilization must compete with an increased potential for drought. Not all plants and crops will benefit. The negative consequences of a changing climate would seem to heavily outweigh any plant-growing benefits.

Finally, a warming climate may affect biomes by changing the mix of plant and animal species. Biomes develop over time as certain kinds of species adapt not only to climate but to one another. If new species are introduced into a biome, the result may be devastating.

Often, the new species acts as an invader, preying on other weaker species or using a disproportionate amount of the available food. Historically, human beings have been the primary, and sometimes accidental, agent in the introduction of invasive plant and animal species. One example of an accidental species invasion is the zebra mussel, which invaded the Great Lakes in the United States in 1986. Since then, it has rapidly spread to other nearby lake and river systems. Biologists think the first zebra mussels accidentally poured into the Great Lakes from water on board a ship that had traveled all the way from the Black Sea, in southwestern Asia. The zebra mussel has since killed off all native mussels in Lake Erie and has caused major damage to pipes and plumbing that draw water from the Great Lakes. Its spread remains uncontrolled.

Global warming may work in the same way. As climate changes, new species are able to spread into once-inhospitable biomes. Beetles and worms that thrive in warm climates have already invaded the taiga forest in Alaska. There, they attack spruce trees weakened from sinking, watery ground and from heavy, branch-breaking winter snowfall. Whole forests have died from the combination of melting permafrost, changing climate, and attacking, invasive insects.

In the next chapter, we look at other ways that biomes are currently reacting to changing climate. Scattered around the world, scientists have observed changes in the distribution of plants and animals in recent years. Most of these changes point to global warming as a cause.

4 Signs of Change

The year 1998 was the warmest year of the warmest decade in a thousand years. An extraordinarily strong El Niño, a warming of ocean water in the tropical eastern Pacific, teamed up with the ongoing warming of the earth's atmosphere. The destructive effects of the unprecedented temperatures reverberated across the ocean biome far beyond the eastern Pacific hotspot.

Worst hit was coral. Coral reefs supply the habitat for an estimated 25 percent of all species found in the ocean biome. The level of species diversity found in a coral reef has been compared to that found in the Amazon rain forest. Coral contains a microscopic algae called zooxanthella. This algae is what gives coral its wide spectrum of color, and it also provides food and oxygen, which help the coral grow. When ocean water becomes too warm, the coral expels its color-giving algae and turns white, or bleaches. Without the algae to provide nutrients, the coral dies.

In 1998, the rising ocean water temperatures struck down some of the world's greatest coral reefs. The Great Barrier Reef along the northeastern coast of Australia suffered its worst bleaching in 700 years. Destructive bleaching also occurred in the Seychelles and Maldives, two Indian Ocean island chains. And off the coast of Belize in the Caribbean Sea, the largest coral reef in the Northern Hemisphere died off in amounts greater than any bleaching event in 3,000 years. Worldwide, some 15 percent of all coral reefs suffered a crippling bout of bleaching in 1998. Only a third of these reefs were able to recover the following year. Because of global warming and rising ocean temperatures, some biologists predict that most remaining coral reefs may be dead in fifty years. Others say as soon as twenty.

Elsewhere in the aquatic biome, there are other signs of changes. In Ireland, striped dolphins have been washing up on the shore in greater and greater numbers. This particular species of dolphin is common in much warmer water farther south, in the Mediterranean Sea. These dolphins were not seen around Ireland before 1985.

In western North America, biologists note significant changes in salmon. The Fraser River, which runs out of the mountains of British Columbia into the Pacific Ocean, is a major salmon breeding ground. In the headwaters, far upstream where salmon spawn,

Rising ocean water temperatures have killed algae and caused destructive coral bleaching at the Great Barrier Reef in Australia.

water temperatures now rise as high as 71°F. That's nearly lethal for salmon. In 1999, the Fraser River Fishery had to be closed for the first time in history as only 3 million of an expected 8.2 million salmon swam upstream from the ocean to the breeding grounds in the headwaters. Scientists attribute this reduction to overfishing, which reduces available nutrients to the remaining salmon, and to cycles of warmer and colder Pacific water that raise or lower the supply of food for the salmon. But climate change, and the increasing river temperatures, may very well be partly to blame.

On land, scientists note changes in the behavior of birds. In America, robins are migrating from lower elevations to higher elevations an average of two weeks earlier than in the mid-1970s. In Europe, the little egret is making inroads into England. Common across continental Europe, it was unknown in England until 1995. As of 2000, there were several hundred breeding pairs in wetlands in the southern part of the country. Farther north, scientists are monitoring the populations of birds in the tundra. According to the World Conservation Monitoring Centre, millions of geese and sandpipers may be endangered by 2100 as the northward-spreading taiga forest biome overtakes the tundra biome. Some species are already endangered.

Other smaller, winged creatures show evidence that global warming is altering grassland and forest biomes. Again in England, scientists observe that the red admiral butterfly is appearing an average of one month earlier in the springtime and is surviving up

Global warming changes the behavior of birds, causing them to migrate to unusual places at different times of the year. Many species of birds may become endangered or extinct as a result.

to eight days longer into autumn. In the United States, a 1996 study by a biologist at the University of Texas detailed changes in the range of the Edith's checkerspot, a butterfly found in the western part of the country. The butterfly was observed at 150 sites from Mexico to Canada over three years in the 1990s. During this time, the biologist noted that the species was becoming extinct in warmer, lower-elevation biomes. Overall, the range of the Edith's checkerspot had moved northward by approximately 100 miles. While global warming was not cited as the specific cause of the shift, the biologist who made the study noted that it is just the kind of change that would be expected as a result of a warming climate.

Changes in the earth's climate affect plant life. As a result of warming temperatures, the famous cherry blossoms in Washington, DC, now bloom an average of one week earlier than they used to.

Plant life also shows evidence of climate change. In Washington, DC, a Smithsonian study documented the shifting dates of the cherry blossom bloom each spring over a span of thirty years. Scientists were surprised to learn that the date of the cherry tree bloom in the nation's capital is an average of one week earlier than it was around 1970. Average minimum temperatures around Washington, DC, during bloom time are up anywhere from one-half to over two degrees. Some of this warming may be attributed to the urban heat island effect, a phenomenon in which air temperatures rise around expanding cities. But observations of plants and trees in nonurban forest biomes show similar changes. The probable culprit is a warming climate.

In New Mexico, environmental scientists have been studying transition zones between temperate forest biomes. These transition zones, known as ecotones, typically contain a mix of species belonging to two different kinds of environments. At the Bandelier National Monument in New Mexico, the ecotone between a pinon-juniper forest and a ponderosa pine forest moved 1.25 miles in just five years, showing just how fast biomes can change. In Ohio, meanwhile, biologists speculate on the rate of subtropical tree migration. The U.S. Forest Service has test-planted subtropical palmettos in Ohio that have survived at least three winters. Southern tree species can migrate northward as much as ten to thirty miles per year. By 2100, palmettos may be growing naturally in parts of the midwestern United States.

It's not just warmer temperatures that may affect plant life. In the Great Plains of the United States, the grassland biome is threatened not only by hot weather but by lack of rainfall. Longer-lasting and more severe droughts in a warmer world may lead to desertification, the process whereby a grassland biome turns into a desert biome. Scientists know that parts of the Great Plains once supported large sand dunes of the kind currently blown by hot winds in the Sahara Desert. These dunes, located in western Nebraska, are now covered by grass and wildflowers and look just like regular hills. But a change to a slightly drier climate in this part of the world could kill off the grass. Winds would then blow the sand anew, in a process similar to that which took place in the southern Plains states during the dust

Global warming may melt glaciers and ice caps, causing ocean levels to rise. As a result, coastal areas, such as this swamp in Louisiana, may become flooded.

bowl of the 1930s. Worldwide, desertification threatens an estimated 40 percent of the world's land surface. Each year, it converts over 55,000 square miles of land into desert, causing billions of dollars in damage and displacing countless thousands of people.

A recent computer prediction showed a similarly drastic turn of events for the Amazon rain forest. Scientists at the Hadley Centre for Climate Prediction and Research in England have run software on large supercomputers that simulates how global warming might affect biomes. If carbon dioxide levels continue to rise at current rates, one supercomputer simulation shows a regional hotspot developing in the northeastern Amazon rain forest. Average temperatures there may rise by more than 10°F, and rainfall may drop off to droughtlike amounts. Scientists say that the predictions amount to an "extreme die-back" as a significant part of the rain forest turns into desert. Computer predictions such as this are prone to error, and by no means should the Hadley computer forecast be counted on as a perfectly accurate vision. Still, it illustrates how a warming planet may have significant consequences for biomes of the future.

Dry or wet, global warming will likely offer changes for all biomes. Coastal biomes can be affected by rising ocean levels. Global warming is predicted to cause an ocean level rise of anywhere from five to over thirty inches. The swelling seas will be the result of melting glaciers and ice caps, and of the expansion of water molecules in the warming oceans. Coastal mangrove swamps, such as those in Bangladesh, may become flooded. Coastal wetlands are particularly fragile, since the level and temperature of the mixing salt water and freshwater is critical to the survival of numerous species.

In this survey of the changing nature of plants and animals around the world, we finally return to the Arctic. Computer predictions show that global warming will have its greatest impact in these northern biomes. And much of the evidence for the current, ongoing transformation of world climate comes from the tundra and the taiga.

Scientists and local residents around Hudson Bay in Canada have recently witnessed changes in the polar bears that live there. Polar bears hunt seal pups on the ice of Hudson Bay in winter. But

Global warming has caused thunderstorms and lightning to invade the northern latitudes, where the aurora borealis shines. Before, the Inuit people of Canada and Alaska had never seen a thunderstorm.

because of global warming, the ice is breaking up and melting an average of three weeks earlier than in 1975. This means that polar bears have that much less time to hunt and eat. As a result, the bears have become fewer in number and thinner. A typical full-grown male polar bear might weigh over 1,300 pounds. Today, their average weight is as much as 130 pounds less than what it should be. Meteorologists at Environment Canada, the Canadian governmental weather forecasting service, speculate that by 2100, Hudson Bay may be mostly ice free. The surrounding taiga forest may change to something more like the temperate forest biome of present-day New England.

In the night sky over extreme northern Canada and Alaska, the aurora borealis shimmers and shines with waving, luminous curtains. It's a silent phenomenon, a natural show of fireworks that has come to be associated with northern regions. But recently, another atmospheric phenomenon has invaded from the south. Crackling lightning and booming thunder have started to pierce the far northern sky. Thunderstorms are a warm-weather phenomenon. The native Inuit people of the far north, having never seen nor heard a thunderstorm, have no word to describe it. Locals report that animals are similarly confused. From drunken forests, to melting glaciers, to thinning polar bears, to thunder and lightning—in these remote, northern locations, the atmosphere seems to be giving its clearest signs that the earth's climate is indeed warming. Biomes appear likely to suffer some of the greatest consequences.

Conclusion

According to the World Wide Fund for Nature, a full one-third of the world's natural habitats are threatened by global warming. Northern biomes, such as tundra and taiga, will experience the greatest change, with possibly up to 70 percent of habitats lost to the drastically changing climate. Across the world, plants and animals will have to adapt and migrate as fast as possible to keep up with shifting weather patterns. In some cases, especially where species are isolated or already threatened, the strain may be too much. Extinction will be the result.

The diversity of life found in the various biomes of the world is more than just an interesting curiosity. Life on Earth has developed into an intricate web of interdependent species. Many of these plant and animal species provide food for humans. Or, if humans don't eat them directly, they are part of the food chain for other plants and animals or are important to us in different ways. Some plants, for example, hold the secrets for lifesaving medicines.

Living organisms develop within biomes in such a way that no one organism overtakes the others. All are able to survive within limits. Global warming threatens to disrupt the natural balance of life found in the various biomes. As the planetary climate changes in the next century, scientists think the average temperature of the earth will rise anywhere from three to as much as eleven degrees. This will result in a change in climate unlike any seen in thousands of years. Changes are already taking place among various kinds of plants and animals all over the world. While global warming may be an accidental outcome of the industrial development of human civilization, it may have disruptive and destructive consequences for the civilization of plants and animals. Our fate is directly linked to the fate of the world's biomes.

Glossary

biome   A community of plants and animals living in a common natural environment. Examples of biomes include rain forest, grassland, desert, and tundra.

bleaching   The process by which coral turns white and begins to die. One cause of bleaching is unusually warm ocean water.

canopy   The layer of treetops that covers a forest.

climate   The average weather conditions over a long period of time, generally decades or more.

computer model Computer simulation of the behavior of the atmosphere and oceans, and how they change over time.

desertification A change in biome from grassland to desert, sometimes caused by severe drought.

ecotone The transition zone between two biomes.

El Niño A warming of ocean water in the tropical eastern Pacific. When El Niño becomes particularly strong, it can affect weather patterns worldwide.

fertilization effect The process by which increasing amounts of carbon dioxide in the atmosphere enhance the natural processes that cause plants to grow.

fossil fuel Any fuel made from the decayed remains of ancient plant life. Includes coal, natural gas, and oil.

global warming The warming of the planet due to increasing amounts of greenhouse gases in the atmosphere.

greenhouse effect The naturally occurring process whereby the earth is warmer than it otherwise would be because of the presence of the atmosphere. Without the greenhouse effect, the earth would be devoid of life. Certain gases, including carbon dioxide, contribute to the greenhouse effect.

greenhouse gas Any gas that efficiently absorbs outgoing radiation from the earth, thereby contributing to the greenhouse effect. The main greenhouse gases are water vapor, carbon dioxide, methane, nitrous oxide, chlorofluorocarbons, and ozone.

Industrial Revolution The rapid growth of factories and industry in the eighteenth and nineteenth centuries, supported by the burning of coal for energy. The onset of the Industrial Revolution led to increasing amounts of carbon dioxide in the atmosphere.

intertropical convergence zone (ITCZ) Zone of unsettled weather in the Tropics extending around the earth near the equator.

permafrost A layer of permanently frozen ground just underneath the surface of the earth; underlies the tundra and much of the taiga.

prairie   A temperate grassland biome characterized by long grass. (Contrast with steppe.)

radiation   Energy in the form of invisible electomagnetic waves that travel at the speed of light.

savanna   A tropical grassland biome.

steppe   A temperate grassland biome characterized by short grass. (Contrast with prairie.)

taiga (also called boreal forest)   The cold, Northern forest biome extending across large parts of Canada, Alaska, Russia, and Scandinavia. The taiga is the largest land-based biome on the planet.

temperate zone   The part of the earth in both the northern and Southern Hemispheres between the colder Arctic and the warmer Tropics.

tundra   The treeless, barren, and cold Arctic biome situated north of the taiga.

For More Information

American Meteorological Society (AMS)
45 Beacon Street
Boston, MA 02108-3693
(617) 227-2425
Web site: http://www.ametsoc.org/AMS
The AMS is the premiere professional
meteorological organization in the
United States.

Environmental Defense
257 Park Avenue South
New York, NY 10010
(212) 505-2100
Web site: http://www.edf.org
The Environmental Defense Web site

contains numerous articles about global warming and its potential effects on the environment.

Weatherwise Magazine
Heldref Publications
1319 Eighteenth Street NW
Washington, DC 20036-1802
(202) 296-6267
Web site: http://www.weatherwise.org
A popular magazine about all things weather-related.
Find it at your local library or newstand.

World Wildlife Fund (WWF)
1250 Twenty-fourth Street NW
P.O. Box 97180
Washington, DC 20037
(800) CALL-WWF (225-5993)
Web site: http://www.panda.org
Web site: http://www.panda.org/kids/kids.htm
Web site: http://www.worldwildlife.org
Web site: http://www.worldwildlife.org/fun/kids.com
The WWF is the world's largest independent conservation organization. Visit its Web site to learn about the effects of climate change on plants and animals, and other environment-related topics.

For Further Reading

Allaby, Michael. *Biomes of the World.* Danbury, CT: Grolier Educational, 1999.

Arnold, Caroline. *El Niño: Stormy Weather for People and Wildlife.* New York: Clarion, 1998.

Chandler, Gary, and Kevin Graham. *Guardians of Wildlife.* New York: Twenty-First Century Books, 1996.

Kaplan, Elizabeth. *Taiga.* New York: Benchmark Books, 1996.

Kaplan, Elizabeth. *Temperate Forest.* New York: Benchmark Books, 1996.

Kaplan, Elizabeth. *The Tundra.* New York: Benchmark Books, 1996.

Patent, Dorothy Hinshaw. *Biodiversity.* New York: Clarion
   Books, 1996.
Phillips, Anne W. *The Ocean.* New York: Crestwood House, 1990.
Ricciuti, Edward R. *Desert.* New York: Benchmark Books, 1996.
Ricciuti, Edward R. *Rainforest.* New York: Marshall
   Cavendish, 1996.
Sayre, April Pulley. *Grassland.* New York: Twenty-First Century
   Books, 1994.
Sayre, April Pulley. *Tundra.* New York: Twenty-First Century
   Books, 1994.
Stevens, William K. *The Change in the Weather: People,
   Weather, and the Science of Climate.* New York: Delacorte
   Press, 1999.

Index

About the Author

Paul Stein has a B.S. in meteorology from Pennsylvania State University. He has eight years' experience as a weather forecaster, most recently as a senior meteorologist for the Weather Channel. Currently, he develops computer systems and software that display and process weather-related data.

Photo Credits

Cover image © Photo Researchers, Inc.: rain forest in Central America.

Cover inset © Robert Simmon, IKONOS data/Space Imaging/NASA Scientific Data Purchase: Amazonia, an area of the Amazon rain forest.

Front and back matter © Animals in Action/Digital Stock: landscape.

Introduction background © Staffan Widstrand/Corbis: glacial landscape of Ellesmere Island.

Chapter 1 background © Corbis: scarlet macaw parrots.

Chapter 2 background © Elements of Nature/Digital Vision: desert dunes.

Chapter 3 background © Jacques Descloitres, MODIS Land Science Team: Alaska as photographed from a satellite.

Chapter 4 background © Scientific Visualization Studio, NASA Goddard Space Flight Center/Landsat Project: a coral reef in Plantation Key, Florida.

P. 6 © FPG; pp. 8, 14, 26 © Elements of Nature/Digital Vision; pp. 12, 33, 36 © Photo Researchers, Inc.; pp. 13, 18, 29, 48 © Pictor; p. 17 © Michael S. Yamashita/Corbis; p. 38 © Kevin Schafer/Corbis; p. 43 © Harvey Lloyd/FPG International; p. 45 © Layne Kennedy/Corbis; p. 46 © Morton Beebe/Corbis; p. 50 © Tim Thompson/Corbis.

Series Design and Layout

Geri Giordano